# Find Your Light!

## Theater is Life.
## Life is Theater.

*by*
**Angela Tortorici Mantero**
*with*
**Anthony J. Tortorici**

Find Your Light!
Theater is Life. Life is Theater.

by Angela Tortorici Mantero
with Anthony J. Tortorici

Copyright © 2024 Bella Dolci LLC

All rights reserved. No part of this publication may be reproduced, distributed, or transmitted in any form or by any means, including photocopying, recording, or other electronic or mechanical methods, without the author's prior written permission, except in the case of brief quotations embodied in critical reviews and certain other non-commercial uses permitted by copyright law. For permission requests, please contact the author.

ISBN Numbers:

Paperback 978-1-917095-08-2 Angela Tortorici Mantero
Hardcover 978-1-917095-09-9 Angela Tortorici Mantero

For Worldwide Distribution

www.FindYourLight.us
AskFindYourLight@gmail.com
www.facebook.com/findyourlighttheaterislife/
Instagram.com/Find_Your_Light_Theater

Bella Dolci LLC
Publishers
Contact: askbelladolci@gmail.com

# Dedication

This book is dedicated to all the players on the world's stage -- especially those in middle schools, high schools, colleges, and community theaters everywhere.

# Acknowledgments

Finding one's light is a daily endeavor. Sometimes, you are on your own, but often there are great people nearby who will point you towards the light.

- My parents, Toni and Tony Tortorici, have always encouraged and supported my theatrical endeavors.

- Susan Pillans, my middle-school English teacher and first director, imprinted a love of theater on my heart.

- Katie Schmitz and Stephanie Stadler, my high school dream team director and choreographer, respectively, allowed me to confidently, if not successfully, try my hand at musical theater – allowing me to discover that my heart (and talent) lies squarely with the play.

- Vincent Paul Murphy, as Artistic Producing Director for Theater Emory at Emory University, took numerous chances on me and taught me to be true to myself whether acting or directing or just being.

- My children -- Marisa, Francisco, Olivia, and Antonio – opened up a whole new world to me, where theater is at once playing, teaching and learning. They allowed me to put my knowledge and love of theater to use in my life as a mother in a unique way that unified our family.

- My husband, Frank, who, while he has never stepped onto a stage, has always appreciated the value of theater as a means to living well.

# Introduction

The theater is often compared to life because it reflects the human experience. Just as in life, the theater presents a wide range of emotions and situations that people can relate to. The stage is a microcosm of the world, where stories unfold and characters interact in ways that mirror real life.

In the theater, as in life, there are heroes and villains, triumphs, and tragedies. The actors portray characters who face challenges and overcome obstacles, just as we do in our daily lives. The drama on stage can inspire us to be better people and to strive for greatness.

The theater also provides an escape from the mundane routine of everyday life. When we enter a theater, we leave our worries at the door and immerse ourselves in a different world. For a few hours, we can forget about our problems and lose ourselves in the story unfolding before us.

But the theater is more than just entertainment. It has the power to educate and enlighten us. Through the stories it tells, the theater can teach us about history, culture, and human nature. It can challenge our beliefs and make us think about important issues.

In many ways, the theater is a reflection of life itself. It presents a microcosm of the world on stage, where we can see ourselves and our experiences reflected at us. The theater has the power to move us, to inspire us, and to teach us about ourselves and the world around us.

In his iconic monologue from Act II/Scene VII of the comedy *As You Like It*, Shakespeare takes the audience on a journey of the complete lifecycle of a human being which begins:

*"All the world's a stage, and all the men and women merely players; they have their exits and their entrances; and one man in his time plays many parts..."*

As Shakespeare created this fitting metaphor, this book - *Find Your Light!* equates the world stage to life itself, finding life lessons in stage directions and other theater references.

# Find Your Light

## Theaterism –

There is always a "hot spot" on stage where the lighting is best. Be aware and position yourself there to be properly illuminated by the stage lighting. You can feel the warmth of the stage light when you're in just the right spot, as opposed to a cooler spot when you're standing outside it.

This is not necessarily a spotlight. This is a subtle space on stage that is lit for the audience to best see what's going on.

Stage lighting is very intentional – shadows and light help to tell the story. This is why it's so important to know where the light is. Most of the time, you should seek out and be in the light.

## Life Lesson –

The "light" you must find is your purpose, your role. Find yourself. Be yourself. You are unique. You are special. You deserve to be the featured player in your life, and you have a role to play in the lives of others.

After all, you are, indeed, a part of everything that's going on in this stage of life. Play your role in the light for everyone to see.

It means to discover and pursue your passions or purpose in life. It involves identifying what brings you joy, fulfillment, and a sense of purpose and direction.

Once you have found your light, you can use it as a guiding force to achieve your goals and serve others.

# Wait in the Wings

## Theaterism –

The wings are the sides offstage where you cannot be seen by the audience. They are where you wait to make an entrance. If you're not on stage, you're waiting to go onstage.

Many actors remain in character when they're waiting in the wings; while this isn't required (though it should be respected by those around them), it is important that you not wait until you're actually in view to be in character.

Be ready; wait for your cue with anticipation and intention; get in character. Be aware of what's going on, on stage and off. Be ready to enter the stage on cue. Don't enter too early and step on someone else's line or interrupt their moment. Don't miss your cue and drag down the energy of the play by creating a lag or silence. Wait for it.

# Life Lesson –

There will be times to be on life's stage and times to be off. Use those off times to increase awareness of your surroundings. Tune in to who's doing what. Think about your goals and how you will reach them. It's planning time. Realize, however, that planning is only that: planning.

Be ready to get back on life's stage and play your part! Be ready for whatever might come your way and seize opportunities.

"Timing is everything." It is in waiting that we learn patience. Waiting for the right moment to act allows our actions to be the most effective.

Life has cues, too. Learn to read the cues around you, know the people around you, and know what's expected of you. Then, you can act appropriately, at the appropriate time, in the appropriate manner.

# Make an Entrance

## Theaterism –

This is the moment you step onto the stage, entering a scene in progress. Sometimes you enter quietly into the background – but sometimes, you take over the whole stage! Know which kind of entrance the moment calls for; this shows respect for what's going on before your entrance and a desire to move the story along authentically.

There is always energy associated with a scene being played out. Be aware of that energy and then either change the energy or match it. If you change the energy, make sure it is relevant to the story and necessary to where it needs to go. In matching the energy, this shows you are sensitive to what's happening in the moment.

## Life Lesson –

Having an understanding of the situation you're entering is valuable in navigating life's experiences.

Don't underestimate the power of your presence to transform a situation. Be mindful of the energy you bring into a room.

Your presence can influence the atmosphere and the experiences of those around you. Aim to radiate positivity, kindness, and empathy, creating a space where others feel uplifted and inspired.

You have the ability to make a difference and be exactly what a situation needs. Embrace that opportunity and create a positive impact.

# Hit Your Mark

## Theaterism –

Know where you're going and move with purpose and intention.

Don't upstage others; know where the focus should be and honor that.

Directors block scenes with intention – allowing for improvisation, of course, but there is always a general design to a scene that the actors should try to maintain. Ignoring this vision throws off the stage picture, creates an imbalance, and confuses (and annoys) the audience.

This also applies to dances – even more so! Choreography provides even more precise stage positions – if you miss your mark, the whole dance could be ruined.

## Life Lesson –

Be <u>where</u> you're supposed to be <u>when</u> you're supposed to be there. Show up on time. Honor your commitments. Know what's expected of you and make good on it.

This doesn't mean you can't be spontaneous, but you should be mindful of your surroundings, self-aware of how your actions may affect those around you.

Be reliable. Be dependable. Be steadfast. These are admirable qualities that others value and which will serve you well in any situation.

# Think on Your Feet

## Theaterism –

Unforeseen circumstances and off-script moments can occur -- an actor may stumble and fall, or someone may miss their cue. In such instances, it is vital to stay in character. To do this, you must possess sufficient knowledge about your role and the narrative. This enables you to swiftly respond or act in a way that maintains the smooth flow of the story.

When faced with unexpected challenges, the goal is to continue telling the story authentically and seamlessly, allowing the performance to progress as planned.

# Life Lesson –

This one seems to have obvious life applications. Forrest Gump said, "Life is like a box of chocolates – you never know what you're gonna get."

Stuff happens. Appointments are missed. Birthdays are forgotten. Fenders are bent.

Life disappoints -- it also surprises pleasantly. Be prepared for either. Know when to say you're sorry if it's your fault. Know when to forgive when it's someone else's.

The best way to be able to "think on your feet" is to know who you are and what story you want your life to tell. When things don't go as planned, when your expectations aren't met, you still have a foundation from which to pivot.

Be ready for anything.

# Ad Lib/Improvise

## Theaterism –

To "ad lib" or "improvise" refers to the act of spontaneously creating dialogue, actions, or content in the moment without prior planning or rehearsal.

Actors may resort to ad-libbing or improvisation if they forget their scripted lines or feel compelled to enhance their performance with additional elements.

This improvisational approach allows them to adapt to unforeseen circumstances, keep the scene alive, or inject spontaneity into their portrayal.

It requires quick thinking, creativity, and a strong understanding of the character and the story.

## Life Lesson –

Life itself is a continuous improvisation as we navigate its unpredictable twists and turns.

While certain moments demand preparation by acquiring knowledge or new skills, our daily interactions with others and the challenges we face often require us to improvise and adapt on the spot.

In our interactions with others, we must be flexible and responsive, adjusting our approach based on the unique circumstances that arise.

# Play to the Back Row

## Theaterism –

Be aware of the entire audience, not just those in the front rows. Each member of the audience deserves to receive the story you're telling.

Volume alone isn't the key; it's about maintaining a posture, keeping your chin up, and directing your gaze just above the last row. By doing so, you fill the entire performance space with your character's presence.

To truly engage the audience, you must be keenly aware of the space in which you're performing. Project your character's energy and emotions throughout the performance space in a way that maintains a genuine connection with the entire audience.

## Life Lesson –

In today's world, the things we say and do tend to last forever. Why? Because they reach everyone, thanks to the internet.

You may only be playing to one person or just a few with what you say and do, but because of the internet, there is no limit to who will hear or see what you are saying and doing. So, be sure that what you say and do are worthy of you forever.

It is said that "integrity is what you do when no one is watching." Be a person of integrity, and you will never have to second-guess yourself or your actions.

And so, "playing to the back row" keeps you aware of everyone, those who are watching and those who aren't.

# Chew the Scenery

## Theaterism –

This means to overact, over emote, or indulge in excessive dramatics so much so that you might think the actor was about to bite chunks out of the set.

Sometimes it's applied as praise, suggesting an actor who is energetic and spirited. However, when an actor engages in scenery chewing, they may overpower the stage, distracting from the focus or even eclipsing the central plot of the play. They are unnecessarily, and annoyingly, distracting.

While passionate acting can be captivating, it is important to demonstrate respect for the collaborative nature of theater and exercise restraint and generosity in a performance.

# Life Lesson –

Exercising self-control in our reactions is a crucial aspect of personal growth and effective communication.

It is important to avoid overreacting, especially in situations where a measured response is more suitable. By practicing self-awareness and considering our surroundings, circumstances, or the individuals involved, we can gauge the appropriate level of reaction.

Strive to strike a balance and avoid escalating the situation unnecessarily. By maintaining composure and thoughtfully expressing ourselves, we foster healthier relationships, navigate conflicts with grace, and create understanding and respect.

# Tell the Story

## Theaterism –

Every individual plays a vital role in weaving together the story of a production. It is crucial to hold the bigger picture in mind as you delve into the intricacies of your character's journey.

Whether you find yourself in a leading role or a supporting one, it is essential to keep your eye on the big picture.

Maintain an awareness of the ensemble around you, acknowledging their significance in shaping the world of the play.

Understanding your place within the story is key. Embrace the interplay between characters, knowing that each person's contribution enriches the collective storytelling experience.

# Life Lesson –

Understand your place in the world! We are all here for a short time to serve a specific purpose! What difference will YOU make in the history of the world?

Every part of your life is its own story – family, friends, school, work, hobbies -- each of those tells a smaller story, which is part of the larger story of your life. Understand your role in each and appreciate the roles of those around you.

Know when it's your story being told, and when it's someone else's. Sometimes, we are the only characters in the story – it's still a story worthy of being written and told!

# Do It The Hundredth Time Like You're Doing it The First Time

## Theaterism –

Theater is repetition. We rehearse over and over again, and then we perform over and over again. There's an opening night, and there is also a closing night. But every night's performance should be consistent.

Remember that it's likely the first time THIS audience has seen something you've already done a hundred times – they deserve the same quality show, the same tried-and-true performance you've been giving all along.

# Life Lesson –

Put your all into all you do. Don't cheat, don't cut corners – you owe it to yourself to be your absolute best!

Be your authentic self, don't be fake. Be consistent, reliable, act with integrity so that others know the real you and they can rely on you.

Being dependable doesn't mean you're not spontaneous and creative. But don't let your spontaneity and creativity come at the expense of being authentic and real. Let people know who you truly are, and let your actions reflect that authenticity.

# Live In The Moment

## Theaterism –

Remain fully present in the unfolding story, the dynamics of your character, and your interactions with the other characters.

Don't let your thoughts wonder beyond the world of the play. Fully immerse yourself in the here and now.

Be present.

By immersing yourself in the present moment, you can fully respond to the nuances of the performance, the reactions of your fellow actors, and the unexpected twists that may arise. Theater thrives on the magic of the present moment.

## Life Lesson −

Embrace the power of being present.

Let go of concerns about the past or anxieties about the future, for the only certainty we have is the present moment.

Be prepared to respond to the needs of those around you.

By immersing yourself in the present, you are able to make meaningful connections, seize opportunities, and experience life to the fullest. Embrace the beauty and unpredictability of the here and now.

# Learn Your Lines

## Theaterism –

In the rehearsal process, the fun really starts once you learn your lines and you're "off book." This is when your character comes alive! You are free to move about the space, gesture with your hands, and move your body in ways you couldn't when you were holding a script.

With the words ingrained in your mind, you can fully immerse yourself in the world of your character.

The deadline to be off-book is a shared responsibility, and everyone in the cast should honor it, out of respect for one another. Even just one person still clinging to the script can slow down the whole production and hold others back from bringing the story fully to life.

# Life Lesson –

Get as much training as you can. School. College. Trade school. Work experience. Recognize your skills and talents and gifts and then hone them. Learn, grow, and always seek to improve yourself and your abilities.

Strive to be your best at whatever you do (not THE best, necessarily, but YOUR best -- there's a difference).

Then, recognize the value your skills, talents, and gifts have for others around you. How can you use them to make a difference for others? There is always someone counting on you to know your stuff, whatever that is!

# Learn Your Cues

## Theaterism –

Cues are other characters' lines or actions that tell you when to speak or move. While it's important to know your own lines and movements, it is equally important to know these cues to make sense of the whole story.

Likewise, know when your line or action is someone else's cue. This is important, so that you don't change or alter your own line or action too much. This could confuse the actor who is relying on you for their cue.

Cues are a two way street – listen for your cue, and give others their cues, and the whole thing works!

# Life Lesson –

Knowing *when* to say something is almost as important as knowing *what* to say in a given situation. That is, know yourself, how you feel, what you think, what you believe – and be able to articulate it, when the time is right.

Conversation builds relationships. This requires listening, but it also requires speaking and sharing. Offering thoughtful comments, posing insightful questions, and displaying genuine interest creates a space where you can learn from others' perspectives and share your own valuable insights and experiences.

# Be Intentional

## Theaterism –

Acting intentionally in the theater means making deliberate choices and executing them with purpose and clarity. It involves understanding the motivations, emotions, and objectives of your character and conveying them authentically to the audience through what you do and say.

By acting intentionally, you create a sense of truth and believability in your performance, There should be a reason for your every movement, a clear motivation for your acting choices.

# Life Lesson –

Acting intentionally in life means making conscious choices and taking deliberate actions aligned with your values, goals, and aspirations.

This requires self-awareness, reflection, and a clear understanding of your priorities. It means taking responsibility for your choices and actively shaping your life according to your desired outcomes.

It involves setting clear goals, making purposeful decisions, and taking proactive steps towards creating the life you envision with a sense of purpose and direction.

# Don't Touch Someone Else's Props

## Theaterism –

The arrangement and placement of props both backstage and onstage are carefully planned to ensure the show goes smoothly.

Each actor bears the responsibility of managing their own props. An actor likely has their own method of preparing for a rehearsal or performance, and ensuring their props are at hand is part of that routine.

Prior to rehearsals or performances, they ensure that their props are precisely positioned as needed. Trusting fellow actors not to touch or move one's props after they've been placed properly is a basic tenet of theater protocol.

## Life Lesson –

Respecting personal boundaries and property is a fundamental principle in life. Common courtesy teaches us not to interfere with or take something that isn't rightfully ours.

Of course, stealing is wrong. But this doesn't just apply to things. Give credit where credit is due. Do not take someone else's ideas as your own.

By honoring this principle, we cultivate trust, integrity, and mutual respect.

# There Are No Small Roles, Only Small Actors

## Theaterism –

What determines the "size" of a role? The number of lines? Time spent on stage? Why do we speak of roles in terms of size? Is it ego?

When directors cast plays, they take the whole production into account. You should presume that the role you were given is the best role for you in this production and then play it to the best of your ability.

A "small" actor allows the "size" of the role to determine how well they play it.

A "big" actor is someone who will take whatever role is given them and make it exactly what it needs to be in the context of the play, ego aside.

# Life Lesson –

Always do your best, no matter what your job is, no matter how big or how small your job is. No matter what task you are given, do it to the best of your ability, with integrity, dedication, and skill.

Do not balk at small tasks or small duties. It doesn't matter if you're working in the mailroom or in the penthouse office as the CEO -- do your best so that you can be proud of the job you've done.

Furthermore, if you're given a task bigger than you thought you could handle, do what's required to rise to the occasion – use it as an opportunity to grow, learn, and become better.

# Suspension of Disbelief

## Theaterism –

Actors often find themselves portraying moments, ideas, and thoughts that seem implausible or absurd. In those instances, even when feeling silly or foolish, the key is wholehearted commitment.

Embrace the reality of the scene by genuinely believing in the moment. By doing so, actors ignite the audience's imagination and guide them into the realm of suspending their disbelief for a time, in order to fully enter the world of the play.

Regardless of the task at hand, within the context of the play, embrace it with unwavering conviction. Infuse each action with authenticity, extending an open invitation to the audience to share in believing the unbelievable.

## Life Lesson –

Believe in yourself, believe in whatever you're going – commit 100% -- and those around you will, too. Mind over matter.

Sometimes, we need to act "as if" before we actually "are." For example, if we act happy, we begin to feel happy.

When we don't feel like doing something, or we don't want to do something, and we do it with a bad attitude, it certainly won't end well.

More often than not, life is a mental game – "it's all in your head" - for better or for worse. So think positive and you will be positive.

# The Show Must Go On

## Theaterism –

"The show must go on" is a popular saying in the theater that reflects the commitment to continue a performance regardless of any unexpected circumstances.

It requires adaptability, quick thinking, and teamwork to overcome obstacles and maintain the momentum of the production.

It represents the indomitable spirit of the performing arts, where creativity and commitment triumph over adversity. The story cannot be told without you! Others depend on you to play your part, no matter what.

## Life Lesson –

The world needs you. The world depends on you. You have a unique purpose that you were made for, and only you can fulfill it.

So, overcome adversity, find strength to persevere . . . because the story of the world around you will be lacking if you don't play your part!

Keep going. Never give up!

# Break a Leg

## Theaterism –

Theater people can be a suspicious bunch! They consider it bad luck to wish someone good luck before a performance, so instead they wish them to "break a leg," believing it will bring the opposite result: a flawless performance.

Its origins are many. In ancient Greece, the audience would stomp their feet instead of clap to show appreciation; if they stomped long and hard enough, they could break a leg. Or, in Elizabethan times, the audience would bang their chairs on the ground, and if they liked it enough, the leg of the chair would break.

But, the most common theory refers to an actor breaking the "leg line" of the stage (see: Offstage). If an actor crossed, or "broke" the leg line, they would get paid for that performance; if they stayed behind the "leg line," they didn't get paid. So, by telling the actor to "break a leg," you are wishing them the opportunity to perform and get paid.

## Life Lesson −

Be encouraging. Support others in their endeavors and wish them well. Wish for their success, and tell them so!

However, in life, you should use precise language, not opposite language as in theater. Saying "Good luck!" or "Congratulations!" costs you nothing, and it builds connection and good will with others.

You never know who needs that affirmation to achieve success. It makes a big difference, so don't hold back on offering words of encouragement and support.

# Places!

## Theaterism –

The call to "places" is given by the stage manager to everyone backstage. It occurs five minutes before the posted curtain time, which is the start of the performance. The proper response of everyone who hears this call is, "thank you, Places!" ensuring the stage manager that the call was heard and the show will start.

This is the moment for everyone to get ready, be in place to start the show, to leave the real word behind and enter the world of the show.

# Life Lesson —

Be ready. Be present. Live in the moment.

Don't miss out on the present moment because you're worried or distracted or doing something you shouldn't be doing.

There is nothing more important than what's happening right now, for the present moment is the only thing you have control over.

Wake up on time.

Show up when you're supposed to.

Honor deadlines.

Pay attention.

# Cast

## Theaterism –

A cast is a group of performers who have been selected to portray the characters in a play, musical, or other production. The cast members work together to bring the story to life and create a cohesive performance.

Performers audition in order to be selected for the cast. Some are chosen, others are not. Sometimes, a performer is asked to be in the cast without having to audition. In either case, the cast is carefully selected, each performer chosen for their particular skills and presence to be the best fit for their role in the overall production.

# Life Lesson -

In life, the "cast" you're a part of comes in many different forms. And each helps tell your story.

Family – you are born into it. Through your common blood, relations, and experiences, this is a bond unlike any other. For better and for worse, they are the first and most important place to find and give acceptance, forgiveness, love, and belonging. They don't always deliver, but the ability is built in, pre-wired, and if everyone works together, the story is told beautifully, if not perfectly.

Friends – you choose them. You may have an entourage, or just a small circle. There is a lot of power and responsibility in choosing your friends. Choose wisely.

Co-workers, roommates, classmates – you are placed among them. You don't often choose these casts of characters. These are usually fleeting relationships, and you may never really click with them. That's ok. Still, they're a part of your story; they will still help you grow, learn, and achieve.

# Character

## Theaterism –

This is the part you play in the production, your role. Characters are defined by their words, actions, and relationships with other characters. You use body language, voice, and facial expressions to bring a character to life on stage.

Once you've been cast as a character, it is your job to find out as much about that character as you can by researching or even creating their backstory through what the character says and what other characters say about them. You cannot act the part authentically without understanding who they are, where they've been, where they're going, and what motivates them. If you need to fill in gaps with imagination and improvisation, make sure it is appropriate to the character as written.

# Life Lesson –

You are the main character in your life story. You have a rich backstory and a bright future ahead of you. Create a strong sense of self. Know who you are, what motivates you, what your strengths and weaknesses are. Be sure to act in a way that is consistent with how you want others to see you.

Use everything that happens to you as an opportunity to learn and grow. Understand how the world around you affects you and forms who you are.

Don't let anyone or anything hold you back from being who you are, and who you strive to be.

# Stars

## Theaterism –

These are actors who have the lead roles in the play. They have significant stage time, carry essential storylines, and become the focal point of the production. It's a big responsibility to be the star, and while it might be an aspiration, it can be very stressful, too.

Because they are more visible and receive more attention, the term can also carry negative connotations, as some stars may develop inflated egos or perceive themselves as superior to their fellow actors.

## Life Lesson –

You are the star of your life's play, without a doubt. Understand that in your life, you play the main role, the biggest role, and don't let anyone take that away from you or make you feel less than insignificant in your own story.

But, remember that it takes the whole cast to tell your story, so treat others well and with respect as they play their part in helping you tell your story. You cannot tell your story without them!

Likewise, discover how you can help others be their best, and strive to be your own best for others. Never belittle those around you in order to build yourself up, Know when to shine brightly as the star of your story and when to be the co-star of someone else's story.

# Co-Stars

## Theaterism –

A co-star is a performer who has a significant supporting role in a play alongside the lead actors. They have less time on stage, but they serve a vital function to the overall story.

Co-stars may bring comic relief or a dramatic turn, helping define the time and place and circumstances of the story. They add tension and depth, they provide insight through their relationships to the lead actors.

Their performance and chemistry with the leads are crucial in creating a compelling and cohesive onstage dynamic.

## Life Lesson –

Understanding when to step back and let others shine is a valuable skill. It doesn't mean quitting or abandoning the story but rather acknowledging the importance of allowing others to take the spotlight.

Additionally, there are times when playing the role of a helper or supporter becomes crucial, uplifting and empowering others.

Recognize that being a co-star can be just as significant as being the star. No one exists in isolation; everyone benefits from having a co-star, someone to walk alongside them.

Embrace your role as a co-star, confident that you are important to someone else's story.

# Chorus

## Theaterism –

The chorus holds a significant role in both Greek and musical theater.

In Greek theater, they serve as the collective voice, expressing the thoughts and emotions of the community and offering moral commentary on the unfolding events.

In musical theater, the chorus enriches the performance with song and dance. These musical interludes can either comment on a moment in time or advance the plot along. The chorus backs up the lead singer in a musical number, providing unity, harmony, and support.

## Life Lesson –

The people we surround ourselves with can have a profound impact on our lives; our own personal "chorus" of friends and companions can influence our journey.

It's important to choose individuals who uplift and inspire us, even if they have different perspectives or backgrounds. They should encourage personal growth, challenge us to reach our potential, and provide support.

Conversely, being surrounded by the wrong people can lead us astray or negatively influence our path. We must be mindful of the company we keep, as it can shape our own reputation and trajectory.

Strive to build a chorus of individuals who align with your values and aspirations, creating a harmonious and supportive network that helps to craft your own story.

# Understudy/Swing

## Theaterism –

An understudy is a performer who is prepared to step into one specific role if the original actor is unable to perform.

The understudy learns the lines, the blocking, and all the nuances of the character, and they are ready to assume the role at a moment's notice. They take on this task with the full knowledge that they may never actually get the opportunity to perform. Nevertheless, the understudy is essential to the production's success, and it is a great honor to be an understudy.

A swing is a highly versatile and adaptable performer who is responsible for learning and performing multiple ensemble or chorus roles, ready to perform any one of those roles at a moment's notice. Their ability to seamlessly transition between different parts is a huge undertaking.

# Life Lesson –

Be prepared to step in and take on a specific task or responsibility when the need arises.

This requires adaptability, versatility, and a willingness to support others in their absence or when they are unable to fulfill their task. Be observant, learning and familiarizing yourself with various skills or knowledge that may be required.

It's about being reliable, dependable, and ready to contribute when called upon, even if it's not your primary task. Be prepared to fill gaps and provide assistance whenever necessary.

Embrace a mindset of continuous learning and being prepared for any situation that comes your way. Be resourceful, resilient, and agile, navigating different challenges and opportunities with grace.

# Ensemble

## Theaterism –

The ensemble refers to a group of performers who work collaboratively to bring a production to life.

Unlike leads or supporting roles, the ensemble functions as a collective entity, often portraying a variety of characters or serving as a backdrop for the main action.

They contribute to the overall aesthetic, energy, and atmosphere of the performance, enhancing storytelling through synchronized movement, harmonized singing, and precise choreography.

The ensemble embodies teamwork and unity. Each member of the ensemble plays an integral part in the production, showcasing their talents while supporting and elevating their fellow performers.

## Life Lesson –

Understanding your importance, even if you're not in the spotlight, means recognizing the value and purpose you bring to any situation.

You contribute to the overall success by providing your own unique support and ability.

Embracing your role in the background shows you know your worth even when you're not the main focus, making a meaningful impact, knowing that your support enables others to shine.

# Ensemble Acting

## Theaterism –

Ensemble acting is a collaborative approach to theater where the emphasis is placed on the collective efforts of the entire cast rather than focusing on individual performances. Roles are often equal in size and prominence.

By putting the needs of the play above personal ego, ensemble actors prioritize the collective success of the production, allowing the story and themes to shine through the ensemble's collective efforts. This approach fosters a deep connection among the performers.

# Life Lesson –

Working together is a fundamental aspect of collaboration. It involves recognizing the importance of collective effort, acknowledging the strengths and contributions of others, and embracing a sense of unity and cooperation.

It requires effective communication, active listening, and the ability to balance individual needs with the needs of the group. Recognizing your strength may compensate for my weakness, and vice versa. Working together cultivates a supportive and inclusive environment where each person's unique talents and perspectives are valued.

# Curtain Call

## Theaterism –

At the end of a performance, the curtain normally closes and the audience begins to applaud. Then, the curtain opens, and the performers come to the front of the stage and bow, receiving that applause as appreciation for their performance.

Its purpose is two-fold. Performers enjoy the adulation and affirmation that they did a good job, and the audience can show their appreciation with applause and congratulatory sounds.

## Life Lesson –

Accept compliments gracefully. And, even if it makes you uncomfortable, do not reject a compliment – to do so is a rejection of the one giving the compliment. A simple, "thank you" is all that is required.

Likewise, be generous in offering praise wherever you can, whenever you find occasion to do so. It costs you nothing, and will likely make the person's day!

# Director

## Theaterism –

The director sets the creative vision and tone of the project. They work with each individual element so that each part adheres to the director's vision for the whole piece.

The director's view of the entire production allows them the unique perspective and authority to guide cast and crew towards a cohesive end. The director works most closely with the cast onstage, but they also communicate with stage management, costumes, light, sound, and set design to bring their unique vision to life.

## Life Lesson –

The director of your life story should be a reliable and trustworthy individual, someone you can turn to when you feel lost or uncertain.

This person may be a parent, teacher, boss, mentor, or even a spiritual guide.

It is essential that this director has your best interests at heart and possesses strong moral values. They should guide you along the right path, leading you towards becoming who you are meant to be.

This director should care deeply about the outcome of your life and be committed to ensuring your journey is safe, authentic, and aligned with your true potential. They are invested in your growth and will provide the necessary support to help you navigate life's challenges while staying true to yourself.

# Coach

## Theaterism –

Not just for sports teams, there are

- Vocal coaches (not to be confused with a voice teacher), who not only help your singing but also how to act your way through a song.
- Movement coaches (not to be confused with a choreographer or dance teacher), who help you learn to use your whole body to create the character and also integrate acting into your dance moves;
- Improv coaches, who help you create from scratch. .

All of these coaches touch on a specific aspect of playing your character, and each can do a lot to help you bring them to life.

## Life Lesson –

Don't be afraid to ask for help, because there are always people willing to teach you.

Embrace the "coaches" who come along at every stage of your life, learn from them, accept what they have to offer you with humility.

Likewise, be willing to share your knowledge with others to help them grow and learn new skills. Don't be afraid to pass on what others have given to you. In giving away what you know, you lose nothing.

"No pain, no gain." In either case, coaching isn't about just praise and encouragement. A good coach will tell you things that may be hard to hear, such as when you're doing something wrong or when you need to work harder to improve. Accept such coaching with humility and as a means to become better.

# Producer

## Theaterism –

The producer oversees every facet of a production, from assembling the creative team and securing funding to managing logistics and marketing strategies. They navigate the intricate balance between artistic vision and financial viability.

A producer must possess a deep understanding of both the artistic and business aspects of theater.

# Life Lesson –

Your life is comprised of many different aspects. Strive to find a balance that nourishes and sustains every area. Give attention to each area of your life in its turn to cultivate a well-rounded and interesting life.

Be organized, be knowledgeable – and most importantly, be patient. Not every action yields immediate results. Allow time for events to unfold and results to take root. By taking charge, planting seeds, and adapting as life unfolds, you can shape your own narrative.

# Angel Investor

## Theaterism –

An Angel investor provides financial support for a production in exchange for a share of the profits.

They willingly take on the risk associated with the uncertainty of the show's success. With a vested interest in every aspect of the production, Angel investors closely monitor the creative process, marketing strategies, and financial management to ensure the best possible outcome.

Their investment helps bring new and innovative theatrical works to the stage, fostering the growth and diversity of the performing arts industry.

## Life Lesson −

Money should be spent wisely, but don't be afraid to take a chance on something you believe in. When you invest in something, take an interest in it and do what you can to help it succeed. Sometimes, you will succeed; sometimes, you won't.

Supporting a passion project means taking a personal interest and actively contributing to its success. Embrace the fact that your investment may not resonate with everyone.

So, understand that something you believe in that's worth investing in may not be embraced by everyone. That doesn't mean you're wrong – it's just a chance you take that others will like and appreciate the same things you do. Don't be afraid to believe in something and run with it.

# Stage Manager

## Theaterism –

The stage manager is in charge of all offstage activity, which includes backstage as well as the light and sound booth.

They are instrumental during the rehearsal process -- recording blocking and other cues, calling forgotten lines when the actors are off-book, organizing set changes and props with the crew, staying close to the director to learn the needs of the show from every angle.

And for performances, they "call" the show -- meaning they give cues for places, set changes, lights, sound, special effects. Essentially, everything that the actors don't do is in the hands of the stage manager, and everyone backstage follows their lead.

## Life Lesson –

Oftentimes, there are people in our lives whose leadership we follow; who have a better grasp on the mechanics of accomplishing a task. They can be a great asset in our growth and development.

But, more often than not, you should take control of your own life. No one is responsible for your actions except you. Know where you're headed, what you want to accomplish, and then make it happen.

Take stock of what you have, what you lack. Determine the best use of what you have, how you can acquire what you need.

Then, set to work putting it all together towards achieving your goal, with all the resources you can muster and by taking control of the situations of your life.

You call the shots. You run the show.

# Set Designer

## Theaterism –

A set designer is responsible for creating the visual environment of a theatrical production. They translate the script into a tangible and immersive stage design, considering elements such as backdrops, platforms, props, and furniture.

They research, sketch, and create detailed plans and models, ensuring that the set is both functional and safe.

The set designer oversees the construction, installation, and dressing (decorating) of the set, working closely with the technical team to bring their design to life on stage.

# Life Lesson –

Creating and organizing your physical space is essential for optimal productivity and a positive mindset.

Whether it's your bedroom, classroom, or workspace, consider its purpose and arrange it accordingly.

A clutter-free and well-organized environment promotes clarity and focus. Transform your space into a welcoming and functional area.

Take ownership of your surroundings and personalize them to reflect your unique style and preferences.

By curating your physical space, you can create an atmosphere that supports your goals and enhances your overall well-being.

# Crew

## Theaterism –

These are the folks who work literally "behind the scenes," running the lights and sound, changing sets, maintaining props, creating costumes. Never seen by the audience, they often receive little recognition or glory, but their expertise and efforts are essential.

Their commitment, technical expertise, and ability to adapt swiftly to any unforeseen circumstances make them an invaluable asset to the production team.

# Life Lesson –

There are always those who tackle the "dirty jobs" which others may shy away from but which are crucial for the functioning of society. Despite being less visible, their work is invaluable and deserves respect and recognition.

You might even find yourself in a similar position someday. Embrace the opportunity to contribute in ways that may go unnoticed. Each individual, regardless of their role, has the power to make a meaningful impact and contribute to the collective narrative of our interconnected lives.

Taking on menial tasks is a testament to your character and sense of responsibility. While these chores may lack glamor or recognition, they are the foundation upon which a well-functioning life is built.

# Auditions

## Theaterism –

An audition is an interview for a particular role or job as a singer, actor, dancer, or musician, consisting of a practical demonstration of the artist's suitability and skill.

An audition is more than just a test; it's a chance to showcase your passion, talent, and dedication. It's the moment where your hard work converges with opportunity.

Prepare well, hone your skills, build a repertoire. Seize that fleeting moment of the audition with confidence and authenticity. Embody the character, let your voice soar, or move with grace and precision.

Auditions are not merely about being chosen; they're about expressing your unique voice and leaving a lasting impression.

## Life Lesson –

You will often have to compete with others who want that same job/show/position.

Recognize your strengths and weaknesses, be honest but confident . . . and then, when you leave the interview, feel satisfied that you did your best, because then it's out of your hands.

Whether or not you get that job/show/position sometimes depends on you, but sometimes it depends on who you're competing against.

Fate plays a part but be sure to do yours – if you want it, make sure THEY know you want it, and let them know why YOU'RE the best person for it.

# Script

## Theaterism –

A script is the written word of the play. It tells what to say (in its dialogue) and where and how to move (in its stage directions). It captures the nuances of each character's journey and the dynamics of their relationships.

The words within a script are carefully chosen by the playwright, carrying the weight of meaning and intention, guiding actors in discovering both character and story. In honor of the playwright's craft, lines should be spoken as written, without taking liberties to paraphrase. Nothing should be added, and nothing should be left out.

Beyond its role in the rehearsal and performance process, a script stands alone as a commentary on the moment in time it encapsulates, free to be interpreted as many times as it is brought to the stage.

## Life Lesson –

Life unfolds without a script, free from preordained lines or stage directions. Each of us is thrust into an uncharted journey, navigating the unpredictable twists and turns of our story.

Unlike a well-crafted script, life is a constant improvisation, requiring us to think on our feet, make choices, and adapt to unforeseen circumstances.

We are the playwrights of our lives, crafting our own storylines, writing our own lines, exploring different roles, discovering our true selves along the way.

It is in this absence of a script that the beauty and spontaneity of life can truly shine.

# Plot

## Theaterism –

The plot is the sequence of events that make up the story. It includes the exposition, rising action, climax, falling action, and resolution.

The exposition is the beginning of the play, where the audience is introduced to the characters and the setting.

The rising action builds tension and leads up to the climax, which is the most intense and dramatic part of the play.

The falling action follows the climax, where the conflicts are resolved, and loose ends are tied up.

The resolution is the end of the play, where the characters are left in a new situation due to the events of the story.

The plot is the backbone of the play, and its structure helps to create a cohesive and engaging story for the audience.

## Life Lesson –

The plot of your life will continue to unfold. Every moment, every day, things will change in this plot.

Pay attention to where it's going, and make sure you stay on track with where you want to be. The plot of your life is a collection of choices, opportunities, and unforeseen circumstances.

Adaptability is key as you navigate the twists and turns, steering towards your desired destination with determination. Don't fear the occasional plot twist; they often lead to remarkable character development, newfound strength and unexpected wonders.

# Dialogue

## Theaterism –

Dialogue is the exchange of words between characters in a story. It reveals their personalities, motivations, and relationships while advancing the plot.

Effective dialogue should sound natural and conversational, capturing nuances of language. It should serve a purpose, providing information, creating tension, or driving the story forward.

Overall, dialogue breathes life into characters, shapes the story, and engages everyone in the journey.

# Life Lesson –

It is said that we have one mouth and two ears because we are supposed to listen twice as much as we speak. So, when entering into dialogue with others, be sure to listen as well as speak. Dialogue is a two-way street.

Dialogue is the dynamic exchange of ideas, emotions, and perspectives through language. It is a vital component of human communication, promoting mutual understanding and empathy. Active listening and respectful responses create an inclusive environment where diverse voices are heard and valued.

Dialogue encourages critical thinking, challenges assumptions, and fosters personal growth. It builds relationships, resolves conflicts, and generates new ideas.

# Monologue

## Theaterism –

A monologue is a solo speech delivered by an actor, uninterrupted, and often directed at an audience or other characters.

Monologues serve to reveal a character's motivations and conflicts. They can be essential for plot development or introduce scenes or acts.

Monologues offer an actor a moment to showcase their talent in a unique way. Every actor loves a good monologue!

# Life Lesson −

Outside of specific contexts like speeches, a monologue in everyday life is not always desirable. It has the potential to dominate a conversation, disregarding the principles of dialogue and active listening. Be mindful not to monopolize a conversation − keep that two-way street of dialogue flowing in both directions.

Similarly, an internal monologue can overrun your thoughts, leading to a loss of control and focus. It is important to maintain a level of mindfulness and self-awareness to prevent thoughts from spiraling out of control and taking over your mood or situation.

Keeping thoughts positive, constructive, and focused is crucial to a healthy state of mind, as allowing negative thoughts to persist can be damaging to your internal peace of mind. Just as one would strive for kindness and respect when conversing with others, it is equally important to cultivate a positive and respectful internal monologue.

# Soliloquy

## Theaterism –

A soliloquy is a compelling theatrical device wherein a character delivers a speech while alone on stage, offering a glimpse into their innermost thoughts, intentions, or motivations.

Unlike a monologue, where the character may address the audience or other characters, a soliloquy is a form of self-reflection.

Soliloquies serve as a powerful tool for playwrights to provide the audience with insights into a character's mind, revealing their true feelings and unspoken emotions.

They offer a window into the character's psyche, allowing the audience to understand their motivations, dilemmas, and conflicts on a deeper level.

# Life Lesson –

Being thoughtful involves engaging in deep contemplation and careful consideration of ideas, decisions, or situations. One effective method to achieve thoughtfulness is by thinking things through. However, there are instances when merely thinking silently may not provide the clarity or perspective needed. In such cases, speaking thoughts aloud can be a valuable tool.

When you verbalize your thoughts, it allows you to externalize and examine them from a different vantage point. As you listen to yourself articulate your thoughts, they can become clearer, helping you gain insights, organize your ideas, and make more informed judgments.

It's a process of enhancing introspection and self-awareness. By evaluating the clarity or rationality of your spoken words, you can fine-tune your thoughts, gain new perspectives, and make more reasoned and sound decisions.

# Act
# (the verb)

## Theaterism –

Acting is an art form that involves embodying a character and bringing them to life on stage. It requires a deep understanding of the script, the character's motivations, and their emotional journey throughout the story.

The actor must convey the character's thoughts, feelings, and experiences through physicality, voice, and facial expressions.

Acting goes beyond mere memorization and recitation of lines. It requires the ability to connect with fellow actors, respond to their cues, and build relationships on stage.

## Life Lesson –

Indeed, you must "act the part," even in life, because everyone has their own character. Be true to yourself and who you are. Only once you know WHO you are can you determine HOW you act to portray yourself (beware, however, that you're not acting someone else's part or trying to be someone else – save that for the stage.)

Being true to yourself means understanding and embracing your own unique qualities, values, and beliefs. It's about being genuine and not trying to imitate or conform to someone else's expectations.

By staying true to your own character, you can navigate life with integrity and confidence, making choices and taking actions that align with your goals.

# Act (the noun)

## Theaterism –

An act is a division or segment of a play that represents a distinct part of the story. It is a structural element that helps organize and pace the overall narrative.

Acts typically mark significant shifts in plot, setting, or time, allowing for breaks in the action and providing natural points for intermission.

Acts help create a sense of rhythm, build suspense, and shape the overall dramatic arc, providing a framework for the audience to engage with the unfolding story.

## Life Lesson –

Life can be seen as a series of acts, each representing a distinct period of growth and development, such as childhood, adolescence, adulthood, and old age.

Each act presents unique challenges, experiences, and opportunities for growth. While some carry expected and cliché experiences, the acts of our life will undoubtedly be full of surprises, twists and turns.

These acts provide structure to our life's narrative, shaping our identities, relationships, and the paths we choose to follow. Oftentimes, these acts are best distinguished in hindsight, as we look back over the past year, or decade, we can see the different acts that have taken shape, molding us into who we are today.

# Intermission

## Theaterism –

Between acts, there is often a brief intermission, when the curtain closes and the house lights come up.

This allows the audience to take a break from the play – to stretch their legs, go to the bathroom, get a snack, or buy a souvenir.

For those involved in the production, it is time to rest, replenish, and fix anything that needs mending, in preparation for the next act.

## Life Lesson –

There are intermissions or breaks between acts in our lives, too. These are time allowing for reflection, learning, and preparation for what lies ahead.

Imagine New Years' Eve, when you review the year you are leaving behind and plan for the year ahead.

Or time between jobs.

Or summer vacation between school years.

Recognize the intermissions in your life, and allow yourself to rest, review, replenish, replace and prepare.

# Costumes

## Theaterism –

Costumes play a vital role in transporting audiences into the world of the story being told. They contribute to the overall atmosphere and help define the personalities, time period, and context of the characters.

Costume designers collaborate with directors, actors, and other production members to bring the envisioned characters to life. They research, sketch, and select fabrics, colors, and styles that align with the artistic vision of the production.

In addition to enhancing the visual aesthetics, costumes also aid actors in embodying their characters. The right costume can inspire movement, posture, and even alter an actor's mindset.

Costumes must work harmoniously with set design, lighting, and sound, to bring the world of the play to life.

## Life Lesson –

Dressing appropriately is not just about adhering to social norms but also about expressing your identity and aspirations.

By dressing in a manner that aligns with your goals and the image you want to project, you can inspire others' confidence in your abilities and enhance your own self-assurance. Your clothing choices send a message about your professionalism, confidence, and attention to detail.

Whether it's dressing for a job interview, a formal event, or simply everyday interactions, the way you present yourself through your clothing can have a significant impact on how you are perceived and the opportunities that come your way. Take pride in your appearance and appreciate what it says about you as a person.

# Special Effects

## Theaterism –

From dazzling lighting effects that create mood and ambiance to visual effects that defy reality to thunderous sound effects that send shivers down the spine, these techniques bring life to the imagination.

These technical marvels are the hidden hands that add enchantment, surprise and wonder to the theatrical experience.

## Life Lesson –

"Fake it 'til you make it" is a mantra that encourages perseverance and self-belief. It emphasizes projecting confidence and determination, even in the face of uncertainty or self-doubt.

It's not about deceiving others or being inauthentic, but rather adopting a positive attitude and taking courageous actions, even when you don't exactly feel it or believe it in the moment.

By embodying the qualities and mindset of success, you can manifest positive outcomes and overcome challenges.

# SRO

## Theaterism –

Standing Room Only (SRO) is a testament to the immense popularity and demand for a show.

When a performance is sold out, eager spectators are willing to stand throughout the entire duration to experience the magic of live theater.

While many assume that a sold-out show means no chance of entry, it's worth checking with the box office for SRO tickets.

## Life Lesson –

In the pursuit of your goals and desires, embrace creativity and resourcefulness. Explore alternative paths and be open to compromises, understanding that flexibility can lead to unexpected opportunities.

Closed doors shouldn't discourage you; there may be another entrance waiting to be discovered.

Don't hesitate to ask for what you want, as you never know what doors may open in response. Persistence can pave the way to achieving your aspirations.

# Flop

## Theaterism –

A "flop" does not earn enough through ticket sales to cover the cost of the production and make a reasonable profit. Specific signs that the play isn't doing well include a failure to fill the theater with paying theater goers, negative reviews in the press, and a decision to close down the production after a relatively short run.

It's important to recognize that a show's success or failure at the box office doesn't necessarily reflect its artistic merit.

Some exceptional productions may struggle due to timing or lack of interest, while mediocre shows may manage to find commercial success.

## Life Lesson −

In your life, you will inevitably experience the flop. You'll attempt something, and you will fail. But, don't give up!

Be prepared for a few flops in your life; just be sure to try for success the next time. Learn from them and try again.

Remember that failure is merely a temporary setback on the path to growth and achievement. Stay determined, adapt, and keep striving for that next triumphant moment.

# Run

## Theaterism –

The duration of a show's performance is known as its run. Some productions have a limited run, with a predetermined timeframe of just a few weeks or even days.

These short-term engagements create a sense of urgency and exclusivity, enticing audiences to experience the show before it closes.

The length of a show's run is influenced by factors such as audience demand, critical reception, financial viability, and logistical considerations. Sometimes, a show's run will be extended because it is so popular; other times, a show may close after a very short run, due to poor ticket sales.

## Life Lesson −

Life is a series of "runs." Moments in time, filled with a purpose.

Seize the moment, regardless of the time constraints. If the time within a given moment is clearly limited, make the most of it.

Recognize each "run" in your life, and make every moment count.

# Onstage

## Theaterism –

"Onstage" refers to the area of the performance space that is visible to the audience.

It is the space where the actors or performers are seen and where the action takes place.

This is where the magic happens -- where everything comes together to tell the story in all its many dimensions.

## Life Lesson –

In life, "onstage" can refer to any situation where an individual or group is in the public eye, being observed by others. It might include situations such as a job interview, a public speaking engagement, a performance, a sporting event.

In general, being onstage implies a level of visibility, scrutiny, and pressure to perform at one's best.

More broadly speaking, being on stage is being alive. It's what you do every day, among friends, family, or co-workers. It's how you behave. Your demeanor. Your talent displayed. Being at your best. Or not.

How you behave onstage is who you are. Be yourself. Be true to yourself.

# Center Stage

## Theaterism –

Center stage refers to the middle area of the performance space. It is an important location on the stage, as it is the focal point of audience attention and allows performers to be seen clearly from all angles.

Center stage is not just a physical location but also a metaphorical representation of significance and prominence. When a performer occupies the center stage, they command attention and hold a pivotal role in the narrative, regardless of their physical location onstage.

## Life Lesson –

Where is the center of your life? More importantly, what's at the center of your life? What or whom is center stage at any given moment in your life story?

Whatever takes center stage in your life needs to be worthwhile to your story. It needs to serve the story you're telling. If it detracts or derails the story of your life, find a way to reclaim center stage.

It shouldn't be trivial nor an obstacle – on the contrary, it should be the main thing, the most important thing, the thing that gives you meaning and purpose.

# Upstage

## Theaterism –

At or towards the back of the stage, away from the audience. The term originated from the use of raked, or sloped, stages where the part of the stage farthest from the audience was higher (upstage) than the part of the stage closest to the audience (downstage).

When a performer is "upstaged," it literally means the downstage player has to turn away from the audience to face the upstage player, so that their back is to the audience.

Figuratively, this means that they have been outperformed or overshadowed by another performer on stage.

## Life Lesson –

Don't overshadow someone else's moment. Don't steal someone else's thunder. Share the moment, or give it to another, but don't take what isn't yours. Remember: "Dimming someone else's light won't make yours shine any brighter."

There's nothing wrong with wanting to be the best, but there's a difference between being your best and overshadowing someone else's best.

When you share the moment with others or give them the chance to shine, you're not only being a good team player, but you're also gaining respect from your peers. Trying to dim someone else's light will only make yours shine dimmer in the end.

# Downstage

## Theaterism –

Downstage is the area of a stage that is closest to the audience. The focal point of a scene is usually played downstage, with background activity played behind it, or upstage.

This means whoever is in the downstage position must be aware of why they're there and what they're doing, because they hold a prominent place on the stage.

Actors who are downstage are closer to the audience and, therefore, more visible.

# Life Lesson –

Being downstage in life means being at the forefront, taking the lead, and understanding why you hold that position.

Often, others follow whoever is in the front. Being at the forefront of any group means leading others by example, first and foremost. Don't ask of others what you're not willing to do, yourself. It translates to having an impactful presence and commanding respect as well as admiration.

Be mindful of whom you're leading, and to where you're leading them. It's a great responsibility.

# Backstage

## Theaterism –

Backstage is like a hidden world within the theater, where the intricate gears of the production turn.

Backstage buzzes with activity as stagehands swiftly maneuver scenery, props, and costumes. Actors get into place or move from stage right to stage left through backstage passageways.

Backstage, there is something called the "leg line." This is an area offstage, marked with a line to let actors know when they become visible to the audience.

Backstage areas are hubs of coordination where the magic of theater is prepared to be presented to the audience.

## Life Lesson –

This can refer to the behind-the-scenes activity of an event or situation, where essential work goes on beyond the public eye; the space where support staff operates, managing tasks which enable the smooth functioning of front-facing roles that directly engage with customers or clients.

It might also be a sanctuary where we retreat to rest and recharge. Where we have the freedom to embrace vulnerability. A place where we confront our fears, address challenges, and make decisions.

Backstage grants us the space to try, fail, and learn from our mistakes without the pressure of judgment.

It's where we refine our skills, nourish our passions, and cultivate our talents to best present ourselves to the world.

# Dressing Room

## Theaterism –

This is the place where actors put on their makeup and costumes to transform into their character. It may be a small private room or a large room for a group.

The dressing room is also a gathering place, a place where actors rest between scenes or prepare for their next entrance. Dressing rooms become sanctuaries for actors to transform into their characters, shedding their own identities.

## Life Lesson –

Everyone needs their own room, the place where you can close the door and find rest and peace. Also where you can get dressed with privacy.

Let your personal space be a sanctuary, a safe space to shed your public persona and just be yourself. To recharge your battery and rest from life's demands.

As this space is probably your bedroom, don't underestimate the importance of a good night's sleep. Our bodies require sleep to function properly, so don't deprive yourself. Set yourself up to sleep well, with dark shades on the windows, calming sounds and smells, a warm blanket and a soft pillow -- and put that phone away!

Surround yourself with things that bring you joy and peace in this space that is all your own.

# Stage Door

## Theaterism –

This is the door at the back or side of a theater, used by performers and theater personnel only.

It is also the place where audience members wait after a performance to meet the actors as they exit the theater. Having shed their costumes and makeup, performers give autographs, take photos with fans, and receive accolades from appreciative patrons. In this way, it is also a verb, "Let's stage-door after the performance and get autographs!" This is a joyful exchange for patrons and performers alike, everyone riding the high from experiencing live theater!

## Life Lesson –

Don't be shy if you want to meet someone. Take a chance and introduce yourself. You never know when you'll meet a new friend, boss or mentor, or make a connection that might help you advance in life.

Be assertive and speak up! With respect, of course, and at the right time, but be your own best advocate, no one can speak for you better than YOU. Make the first move, extend that hand for a handshake. Pay someone a compliment, not just about their physical appearance, but for something they did or can do.

The best part of life is making connections, building relationships, and sharing the journey with others.

# The Fourth Wall

## Theaterism –

The "fourth wall" refers to an imaginary barrier that separates the actors on stage from the audience. It creates an invisible boundary between the fictional world of the play and the real world of the viewers.

The term originated from the proscenium stage, where the stage is framed by three physical walls, and the fourth wall is the one that "opens" to the audience.

Breaking the fourth wall occurs when actors acknowledge the presence of the audience, either by looking at them, speaking directly to them, or interacting with them. This should never be done unless it is a part of the production. Maintaining the fourth wall is a basic tenet of acting.

## Life Lesson –

It is not always necessary to seek validation or approval from others as you make your way through life.

While it's important to acknowledge the presence and impact of others in your life, ultimately, their opinions and judgments should not dictate your choices.

Form your conscience well. Seek guidance from trusted sources. Then trust your instincts, follow your intuition, and have confidence in your ability to make the right choices.

# Dress Rehearsal

## Theaterism –

In the final stages before the show's opening, marking the inclusion of full costumes and makeup. This is the moment the actor is fully immersed in their character, as the physical elements sync with the emotional.

Occasionally, an audience may be present, aware that the production is still fine-tuning its details, forgiving of any mistakes or imperfections.

This crucial phase allows the cast and crew to identify and address any last-minute challenges, and it unites the many elements of the production.

# Life Lesson –

While it is true that life is not a dress rehearsal, it is essential to recognize the value of preparation. In the face of significant events, meticulous preparation becomes paramount, leaving nothing to chance within your control.

Acknowledging that life will inevitably present its challenges, it is crucial to equip yourself with the necessary tools and knowledge to navigate them effectively.

Embrace the mindset of being prepared for whatever comes your way.

Furthermore, the concept of "dressing for the part" extends beyond physical appearance. It encompasses aligning your mindset, attitude, and actions with your goals and aspirations.

# Tech Week

## Theaterism –

This pivotal week signifies the culmination of all production elements -- from music to lights and sound, set, props and costumes. Every component is integrated.

This intense week, often accompanied by late nights, marks the transition from "creating" to "fine tuning." Although the process may prove tedious and exasperating, it is essential to bringing the whole show to life. There is a magical moment as each of the different elements falls into place – it can be the best part of the whole process.

# Life Lesson –

In the tapestry of life's endeavors, our individual actions form mere threads within the grand design. To truly thrive, we must embrace collaboration, uniting with others who contribute their unique talents for the greater good. In this collective journey, adjustments often become necessary, allowing space for someone else's piece to fit seamlessly.

Being flexible, patient, and collaborative are essential qualities.

By fostering a spirit of collaboration, we open ourselves to the richness that emerges from collective creativity and cooperation. Each contribution, no matter how small, interweaves to form a tapestry of shared achievements.

# Performance

## Theaterism –

The finished product, the moment of truth, what it's all been about: months of work, planning, rehearsing, building, gathering, and preparing, all for this moment.

The performance is the thing, as they say. And, while we shouldn't compromise the process for the product, performance is, after all, what theater is about. It's what we do; we give the show to the audience through performance. We tell the story; we give it away as a gift.

And so, even though we have rehearsed for months, we have said the words and sung the songs and danced the dances and changed the sets countless times, it is the audience's first time seeing and hearing any of it.

So, the performance must be offered to each audience as if it's for them alone. In performing, every element has one great responsibility: to tell the story.

# Life Lesson –

Life itself is our performance. But we are not pretending or assuming a role; instead, we authentically embody our part, sharing our true selves and personal journey.

With this understanding, we are prompted to make the most of the singular existence we have been granted. Each moment is an opportunity to deliver our performance with passion, purpose, and integrity.

By embracing this mindset, we strive to live fully, embracing the challenges, triumphs, and growth that come with our individual stories.

# Ghost Light

## Theaterism –

A ghost light is an electric light that is left energized on the stage of a theater when the theater is unoccupied and would otherwise be completely dark.

It typically consists of an exposed bulb mounted in a wire cage on a portable light stand. It is usually placed near the center stage.

The practical use of a ghost light is mainly for safety, enabling you to navigate the theater to find the lighting control console and to avoid accidents such as falling into the orchestra pit and stepping on or tripping over set pieces.

## Life Lesson –

The brilliance of your light is not determined by its grandeur but by the influence it has on others.

Be a light, offering maximum comfort, guidance, and encouragement to those in distress. Your authentic care and support can illuminate even the deepest shadows, spreading warmth, hope, and inspiration.

Allow your light to shine radiantly, illuminating the path for others to discover their way forward.

When faced with challenges and darkness, let your light shine even brighter. In times of adversity, your unwavering positivity and resilience can serve as a beacon of hope for others.

# You can leave the stage, but the stage never leaves you!

Theater is life re-lived.

You can learn something from every show of which you are a part, regardless of your role, whether it is as a performer, stagehand, lighting engineer, or ticket-taker. The artistic process can also teach you a lot about life and how to live it. So, while you may leave theater behind, you will always take the lessons and experiences with you.

Theater folk, by the nature of their craft, are more aware of the world around them: the people, the space, the situations. They have a special understanding of the many facets, twists, and turns of life because they've already lived so many different lives on the stage.

Theater and life are interconnected, each reflecting and influencing the other. Theater reflects life by exploring universal themes, human emotions, and the complexities of relationships.

It holds a mirror to society, shedding light on societal issues and provoking thought and empathy. Similarly, life reflects theater as individuals navigate their own narratives, taking on different roles, facing conflicts, and experiencing personal growth.

Theater serves as a powerful metaphor for life's ups and downs, offering insights, catharsis, and a deeper understanding of the human experience.

Welcome to the stage! Welcome to life!

# About the Author

After spending every possible moment in a theater space throughout high school and college, I left it all behind to get married and start a family, wondering what I would ever do with all my theater experience, never expecting to actually use it for anything of consequence in my life.

Well, after almost 20 years of working with middle school and high school theater, it's clear to me that theater impacts life far beyond the stage.

Now, as an adjudicator for two regional award programs for high school theater, I travel all over Connecticut seeing upwards of two dozen shows each year. The level of talent, experience and resources varies greatly. But, the one thing that is consistently abundant is the courage and creativity of kids becoming and doing more than they ever thought they could and having the time of their lives.

Writing "Find Your Light! Theater is Life. Life is Theater" with my father has been an unexpected and gratifying culmination of sharing my passion for theater with others. These theater lessons have helped me live a better life. I hope they do the same for you.

~ **Angela Tortorici Mantero**, *Author*

# Index

About the Author, 134
Acknowledgments, 4
Act (the noun), 94
Act (the verb), 92
Ad Lib/Improvise, 18
Angel Investor, 72
Auditions, 80
Backstage, 116, 117
Be Intentional, 34
Break a Leg, 44
Cast, 30, 38, 48, 49, 50, 53, 62, 66, 124
Center stage, 110, 111, 130
Character, 10, 16, 18, 20, 24, 28, 30, 34, 50, 51, 58, 68, 79, 80, 82, 85, 88, 90, 92, 93, 118, 124
Chew the Scenery, 22
Chorus, 56, 57, 58
Coach, 68
Copyright, 2
Co-Stars, 54
Costumes, 66, 78, 98, 116, 118, 120, 124, 126
Crew, 66, 74, 124
Curtain Call, 64
Dedication, 3
Dialogue, 18, 82, 86, 87, 89
Director, 4, 66, 67, 74
Do It The Hundreth Time, 26
Don't touch someone else's props,, 36
Downstage, 112, 114, 115
Dress Rehearsal, 124
Dressing Room, 118
Ensemble, 24, 58, 60, 62
Ensemble acting, 62
Find Your Light, 5, 2, 7, 8, 134
Flop, 104, 105

Fourth wall, 122
Ghost light, 130
Hit Your Mark, 14
Intermission, 94, 96
Introduction, 6
Learn Your Cues, 32
Learn your lines, 30
Leave the stage, 132
Live In The Moment, 28
Make an entrance, 10
Monologue, 7, 88, 89, 90
No Small Roles, 38
Onstage, 108
Performance, 16, 18, 20, 22, 26, 28, 34, 36, 42, 44, 46, 48, 54, 56, 60, 64, 82, 102, 106, 108, 109, 110, 120, 128, 129
Places, 46, 74
Play to the Back Row, 20
Plot, 22, 56, 84, 85, 86, 88, 94
Producer, 70
Publishers, 2
Run, 73, 75, 104, 106, 107
Script, 16, 30, 76, 82, 83, 92
Set designer, 76
Show must go on, 42
Soliloquy, 90
Special Effects, 100
SRO, 102
Stage Manager, 46, 74
Stars, 52
Suspension of Disbelief, 40
Tech Week, 126
Tell the Story, 24
Think on Your Feet, 16
Understudy/Swing, 58
Upstage, 14, 112, 114
Wait in the Wings, 10

www.ingramcontent.com/pod-product-compliance
Lightning Source LLC
Chambersburg PA
CBHW041318110526
44591CB00021B/2825